Copyright © 1976 Lion Publishing
121 High Street, Berkhamsted, Herts

First edition 1976

ISBN 0 85648 055 X

Photographs on pages 15, 23, 41 and 45 by Phil
Manning; all others by David Alexander

Quotations from the New Testament and Psalms from
Today's English Version, copyright 1966 and 1970
the American Bible Society. Old Testament quotations
from The New English Bible copyright 1970 the
Bible Societies with Oxford and Cambridge
University Presses.

Printed in Great Britain by Purnell and Sons Ltd,
Paulton

A word
of hope

NEW EVERY MORNING

All this I take to heart
and therefore I will wait patiently:
the Lord's true love is surely not spent,
nor has his compassion failed;
they are new every morning,
so great is his constancy.
The Lord, I say, is all that I have;
therefore I will wait for him patiently.
The Lord is good to those who look for him,
to all who seek him;
it is good to wait in patience . . .

LAMENTATIONS 3: 21-26

REJOICING IN HOPE

Now that we have been put right with God through faith, we have peace with God through our Lord Jesus Christ. He has brought us, by faith, into the grace of God in which we now stand. We rejoice, then, in the hope we have of sharing God's glory! And we also rejoice in our troubles, for we know that trouble produces endurance, endurance brings God's approval, and his approval creates hope. This hope does not disappoint us, for God has poured out his love into our hearts by means of the Holy Spirit, who is God's gift to us.

ROMANS 5: 1-5

WE SHALL SEE GOD

O that my words might be inscribed,
O that they might be engraved in an
inscription,
cut with an iron tool and filled with lead
to be a witness in hard rock!
But in my heart I know that my vindicator
lives
and that he will rise last to speak in court;
and I shall discern my witness standing at
my side
and see my defending counsel, even God
himself,
whom I shall see with my own eyes,
I myself and no other.

JOB 19: 23-27

OUR GUARANTEE

If Christ has not been raised from death, then we have nothing to preach, and you have nothing to believe. More than that, we are shown to be lying against God, because we said of him that he raised Christ from death—but he did not raise him, if it is true that the dead are not raised to life. For if the dead are not raised, neither has Christ been raised. And if Christ has not been raised, then your faith is a delusion and you are still lost in your sins. It would also mean that the believers in Christ who have died are lost. If our hope in Christ is good for this life only, and no more, then we deserve more pity than anyone else in all the world.

But the truth is that Christ has been raised from death, as the guarantee that those who sleep in death will also be raised.

1 CORINTHIANS 15: 14-20

THE SOURCE OF HOPE

May God, the source of hope, fill you with all joy and peace by means of your faith in him, so that your hope will continue to grow by the power of the Holy Spirit.

ROMANS 15: 13

WHOEVER BELIEVES WILL LIVE

Jesus said:
'I am the resurrection and the life. Whoever believes in me will live, even though he dies; and whoever lives and believes in me will never die.'

JOHN 11: 25-26

TRUST IN GOD

I depend on God alone;
I put my hope in him.
He alone is my protector and Saviour;
he is my defender,
and I shall never be defeated.
My salvation and honour depend on God:
he is my strong protector;
he is my shelter.
My people, trust in God at all times!
Tell him all your troubles,
because he is our refuge.

Men are like a puff of breath;
mortal men are worthless.
Put them on the scales and they weigh
nothing;
they are lighter than a mere breath.
Don't put your trust in violence;
don't hope to gain anything by robbery;
even if your riches increase,
don't depend on them.

PSALM 62: 5-10

NEW LIFE

Let us give thanks to the God and Father of our Lord Jesus Christ! Because of his great mercy, he gave us new life by raising Jesus Christ from the dead. This fills us with a living hope, and so we look forward to possess the rich blessings that God keeps for his people. He keeps them for you in heaven, where they cannot decay or spoil or fade away. They are for you, who through faith are kept safe by God's power, as you wait for the salvation which is ready to be revealed at the end of time.

1 PETER 1: 3-7

GOD'S PROMISE

Show me how much you love me, Lord,
and save me according to your promise.
Then I can answer those who insult me,
because I trust in your word.
Enable me to speak the true message at all
times,
because my hope is in your judgements.
I will always obey your law,
for ever and ever!
I will live in complete freedom,
because I have tried to obey your rules.
I will announce your commands to kings,
and I will not be ashamed.
I find pleasure in obeying your
commandments;
I will meditate on your instructions.

Remember your promise to me, your
servant;
it has given me hope.
Even in my suffering I was comforted,
because your promise gave me life.

PSALM 119: 41-50

OUR GLORIOUS FREEDOM

I consider that what we suffer at this present
time cannot be compared at all with the
glory that is going to be revealed to us. All
of creation waits with eager longing for God
to reveal his sons. For creation was
condemned to become worthless, not of its
own will, but because God willed it to be so.
Yet there was this hope: that creation itself
would one day be set free from its slavery to
decay, and share the glorious freedom of the
children of God.

ROMANS 8: 18-21

STREAMS IN THE DESERT

Let the wilderness and the thirsty land be
glad,
let the desert rejoice and burst into flower.
Let it flower with fields of asphodel,
let it rejoice and shout for joy.
The glory of Lebanon is given to it,
the splendour too of Carmel and Sharon;
these shall see the glory of the Lord, the
splendour of our God.

Strengthen the feeble arms,
steady the tottering knees;
say to the anxious, Be strong and fear not.
See, your God comes with vengeance,
with dread retribution he comes to save you.
Then shall blind men's eyes be opened,
and the ears of the deaf unstopped.
Then shall the lame man leap like a deer,
and the tongue of the dumb shout aloud . . .
and the Lord's redeemed shall come home;
they shall enter Zion with shouts of
triumph,
crowned with everlasting gladness.
Gladness and joy shall be their escort,
and suffering and weariness shall flee away.

ISAIAH 35: 1-6, 10

THE LIVING GOD

As a deer longs for a stream of cool water,
so I long for you, God.
I thirst for you, the living God;
when can I go and worship in your
presence?
Day and night I cry,
and tears are my only food;
all the time my enemies ask me,
'Where is your God?'

My heart breaks when I remember the past,
when I went with the crowds to the house of
God,
and led them as they walked along,
a happy crowd, singing and shouting praise
to God.
Why am I so sad?
Why am I troubled?
I will put my hope in God,
and once again I will praise him,
my Saviour and my God.

PSALM 42: 1-5

ABSOLUTELY SURE

Abraham believed and hoped, when there was no hope, and so became 'the father of many nations.' Just as the scripture says, 'Your descendants will be this many.'

He was almost one hundred years old; but his faith did not weaken when he thought of his body, which was already practically dead, or of the fact that Sarah could not have children.

His faith did not leave him, and he did not doubt God's promise; his faith filled him with power, and he gave praise to God. For he was absolutely sure that God would be able to do what he had promised.

ROMANS 4: 18-21

GOD'S CHILDREN

See how much the Father has loved us! His love is so great that we are called God's children—and so, in fact, we are. This is why the world does not know us: it has not known God. My dear friends, we are now God's children, but it is not yet clear what we shall become. But this we know: when Christ appears, we shall become like him, because we shall see him as he really is. Everyone who has this hope in Christ keeps himself pure, just as Christ is pure.

1 JOHN 3: 1-3

GOD'S CONSTANT LOVE

The Lord watches over those who fear him,
those who trust in his constant love.
He saves them from death;
he keeps them alive in times of famine.

We put our hope in the Lord;
he is our helper and protector.
We are glad because of him;
we trust in his holy name.

May your constant love be with us, Lord,
as we put our hope in you.

PSALM 33: 18-22

34

FULL OF COURAGE

May our Lord Jesus Christ himself, and God our Father, who loved us and in his grace gave us eternal courage and a good hope, fill your hearts with courage and make you strong to do and say all that is good.

2 THESSALONIANS 2: 16-17

'LET HOPE KEEP YOU JOYFUL'

Love must be completely sincere. Hate what is evil, hold on to what is good. Love one another warmly as brothers in Christ, and be eager to show respect for one another. Work hard, and do not be lazy. Serve the Lord with a heart full of devotion. Let your hope keep you joyful, be patient in your troubles, and pray at all times.

ROMANS 12:9-12

OUR EVERLASTING LIGHT

For bronze I will bring you gold
and for iron I will bring silver,
bronze for timber and iron for stone;
and I will make your government be peace
and righteousness rule over you.
The sound of violence shall be heard no
longer in your land,
or ruin and devastation within your borders;
But you shall call your walls Deliverance
and your gates Praise.

The sun shall no longer be your light by
day,
nor the moon shine on you when evening
falls;
the Lord shall be your everlasting light,
your God shall be your glory.
Never again shall your sun set
nor your moon withdraw her light;
but the Lord shall be your everlasting light
and the days of your mourning shall be
ended.

ISAIAH 60: 17-20

DO NOT BE SAD

We want you to know the truth about those who have died, so that you will not be sad, as are those who have no hope. We believe that Jesus died and rose again; so we believe that God will bring with Jesus those who have died believing in him.

For this is the Lord's teaching, we tell you: we who are alive on the day the Lord comes will not go ahead of those who have died. There will be a shout of command, the archangel's voice, the sound of God's trumpet, and the Lord himself will come down from heaven! Those who have died believing in Christ will be raised to life first; then we who are living at that time will be gathered up along with them in the clouds to meet the Lord in the air. And so we will be always with the Lord. Therefore cheer each other up with these words.

1 THESSALONIANS 4: 13-18

NO MORE TEARS

He will swallow up death for ever.
Then the Lord God will wipe away the tears
from every face
and remove the reproach of his people from
the whole earth.
The Lord has spoken.

On that day men will say,
See, this is our God
for whom we have waited to deliver us;
this is the Lord for whom we have waited;
let us rejoice and exult in his deliverance.

ISAIAH 25: 8-9